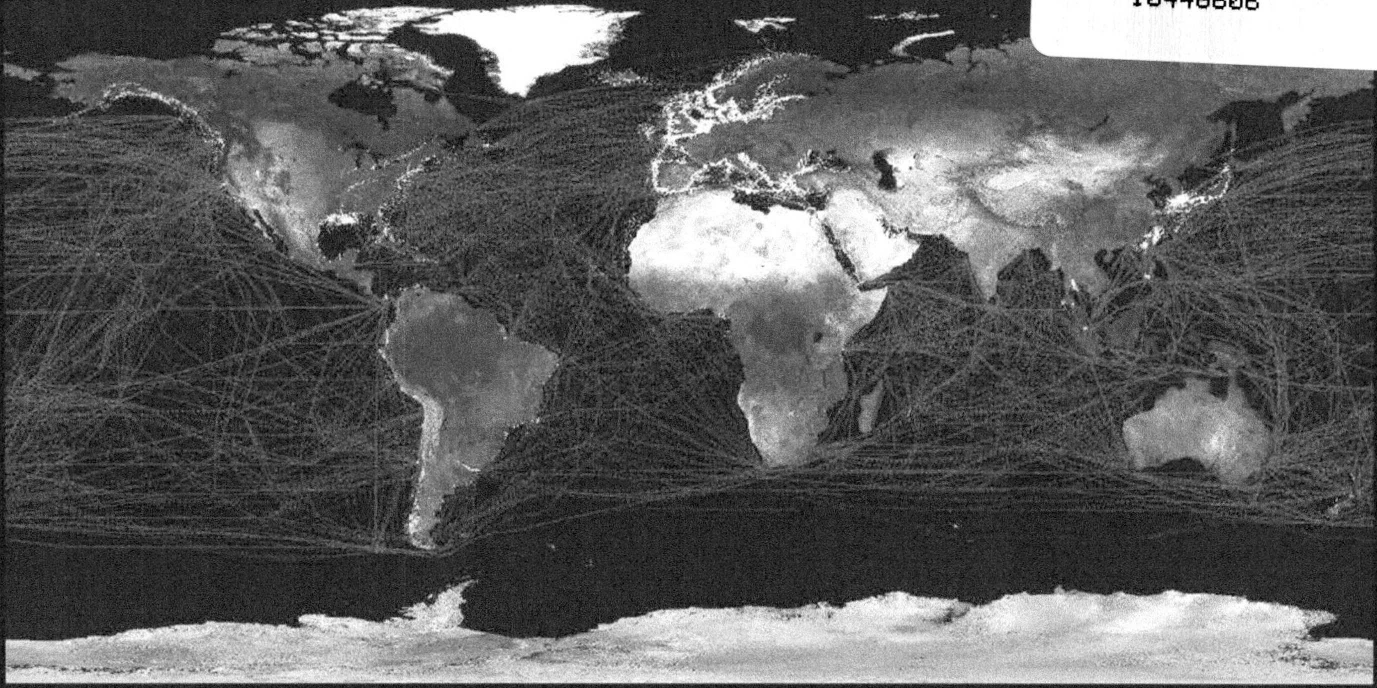

NATIONAL
MARITIME DOMAIN AWARENESS
PLAN

FOR

THE NATIONAL STRATEGY FOR MARITIME SECURITY

DECEMBER 2013

Consistent with Presidential Policy Directive 18: *Maritime Security* (PPD-18) and the *National Strategy for Maritime Security* (NSMS), the *National Maritime Domain Awareness Plan* (NMDAP) merges and supersedes the *National Plan to Achieve Maritime Domain Awareness* of 2005 and the *Global Maritime Intelligence Integration Plan* of 2005. It establishes the foundation for the effective understanding of potential and actual maritime threats and challenges by promoting favorable conditions for integrating and sharing information, including intelligence, to inform decision-makers.

The NSMS is now supported by seven mutually reinforcing implementation plans:

- **The National Maritime Domain Awareness Plan** provides the framework for collaboration to appropriately share and safeguard information within the Global Maritime Community of Interest to position decision-makers to prepare for, prevent, respond to, and recover from a broad spectrum of potential maritime related threats.
- **The Maritime Operational Threat Response Plan** facilitates a coordinated U.S. government response to threats against the United States and its interests in the maritime domain by establishing roles and responsibilities, which enable the government to respond quickly and decisively.
- **The International Outreach and Coordination Strategy** provides a framework to coordinate all maritime security initiatives undertaken with foreign governments and international organizations and to solicit international support for enhanced maritime security.
- **The Maritime Infrastructure Recovery Plan** recommends standardized procedures for restoring maritime transportation systems following an incident of national significance.
- **The Maritime Transportation System Security Plan** provides strategic recommendations to holistically improve Maritime Transportation System security.
- **The Maritime Commerce Security Plan** establishes a comprehensive plan to secure the maritime supply chain.
- **The Domestic Outreach Plan** seeks non-Federal input to assist with developing and implementing maritime security policies.

Although these plans address different aspects of maritime security, they link and reinforce each other. Together, the NSMS and its supporting plans represent a comprehensive national effort to promote global economic stability, protect legitimate activities, mitigate the effects of natural disasters, and prevent hostile and illegal acts affecting the maritime domain. These plans do not alter existing constitutional or statutory authorities or responsibilities of department and agency heads to carry out operational activities or to exchange information. The Maritime Security Interagency Policy Committee (MSIPC), its successor, or its designated representative, will review the NMDAP upon significant changes to PPD-18 or the NSMS or every five years, whichever occurs first. The Maritime Domain Awareness (MDA) Executive Steering Committee (ESC) may modify the NMDAP appendices as required.

EXECUTIVE SUMMARY

> *"The deliberate misuse of the maritime domain to commit harmful, hostile, or unlawful acts, including those against the maritime transportation system, remains an enduring threat to the safety and security of the American people, to wider U.S. national security interests, and to the interests of our international allies and private sector partners."*[1]

Maritime Domain Awareness (MDA) is the effective understanding of anything associated with the maritime domain that could impact the security, safety, economy, or environment of the United States.

The **Maritime Domain** is all areas and things of, on, under, relating to, adjacent to, or bordering on a sea, ocean, or other navigable waterway, including all maritime-related activities, infrastructure, people, cargo, vessels, and other conveyances.

This Plan provides the context to understand the importance of MDA to maritime security and why it is imperative to enhance MDA. It will empower the U.S. Government to understand the characteristics of the current maritime domain, identify the strategic approach we seek to employ, clarify our strategic and foundational priorities, and develop an implementation plan to improve MDA that enables decision-makers to perform their responsibilities consistent with Presidential Policy Directive 18 (PPD-18) and the National Strategy for Maritime Security (NSMS).

This Plan promotes sustaining favorable conditions for global maritime security and prosperity. This is accomplished through the effective understanding of the maritime domain and by improving our ability to appropriately share maritime information, including intelligence, law enforcement information, and all-source data from the public and private sectors. The concept of maritime intelligence integration serves as a foundational and, therefore, necessary priority for the effective understanding of the maritime domain. This Plan serves to unify and support efforts to enhance domain awareness, advance decision-making, and provide the best possible setting to make maritime information appropriately available to all members of the Global Maritime Community of Interest (GMCOI). Additionally, this Plan acknowledges fiscal constraints and establishes priorities of effort consistent with those constraints.

This Plan provides a collaborative framework for the GMCOI to accomplish the following objectives:

- **Organize stakeholders through governance**. Proper governance to coordinate Federal maritime stakeholder activities will promote an interagency shared perspective, which will acknowledge and balance the equities of Federal, as well as state, local, tribal, territorial (S/L/T/T), academic, private sector, and international maritime stakeholders;

---

[1] Presidential Policy Directive 18 (PPD-18): *Maritime Security*, p. 2 (August 14, 2012).

- **Continue to mitigate MDA challenges**. This Plan acknowledges previous work to identify MDA challenges, promotes the development of metrics to understand when a challenge has been addressed or mitigated, and advocates the continued development of solutions to address those challenges. The Plan also recognizes that new and emerging challenges continue to present themselves, validating the requirement for a continuous reassessment process using risk management methodologies;

- **Improve Domain Awareness through enterprise-level access to data.** This Plan promotes maritime information sharing by transitioning from organization-centric databases to web-centric enterprise services that retrieve data from multiple sources (e.g., clouds, databases). This shift provides authorized users with more flexible access to a greater number of sources, types, and volume of data, and the ability to search databases without relying on point-to-point access. Data, under this construct, should be authoritative and conform to recognized standards, such as those currently employed under the National Information Exchange Model (NIEM); and,

- **Enhance collaboration through outreach.** This Plan encourages broad interaction to identify organizations, partnerships, best practices, and other efforts that enhance maritime security through expanded MDA collaboration between the GMCOI members. By collaborating on MDA initiatives and incorporating Federal, S/L/T/T, academic, private, and international maritime partners, this Plan will support and improve interagency capabilities to effectively share information on people, cargo, vessels, infrastructure, natural and man-made disasters, and other potential threats within the maritime domain.

These objectives serve to achieve the following goals:

- Enhance transparency in the maritime domain to detect, deter, and defeat threats as early as possible;
- Enable accurate, dynamic, and confident decisions and responses to the full spectrum of maritime threats and challenges through information sharing and safeguarding;
- Further partnerships to promote and facilitate maritime domain information sharing, safeguarding, and integration; and
- Preserve our Nation's rights, freedoms of navigation and over-flight, and uses of the sea and airspace recognized under international law while promoting the lawful, continuous, and efficient flow of commerce.

As we strive to achieve the above MDA objectives and goals, we must keep in mind the following MDA core principles:

- **Promote Unity of Effort** across the GMCOI;
- **Foster Information Sharing and Safeguarding** using enterprise architecture with partners who have validated appropriate access; and,

- **Ensure Safe and Efficient Flow of Legitimate Commerce** through the recognition that maritime and economic security are mutually reinforcing.

Ultimately, MDA promotes proper risk management planning, enabling the entire maritime community to develop a shared understanding of the potential risks and opportunities for those who wish to harm or disrupt vessels, people, cargo, infrastructure, and resources within the maritime domain.

Underpinning our ability to understand the maritime domain, determine potential threats, and enhance effective decision-making is our ability to integrate maritime intelligence. A coordinated and synchronized intelligence enterprise is a priority for effective security efforts across the maritime domain. To maximize MDA, the U.S. Government must leverage and integrate the diverse expertise of the intelligence and law enforcement communities for a global maritime intelligence capability, according to established statutes and policy.

Together, as we execute the NMDAP, we will harness our collective understanding of the maritime domain; develop and coordinate information vital to our maritime security to make it available, discoverable, and retrievable by authorized users; and assist those charged with preserving the security of our Nation. Ultimately, the backbone of protecting the United States, its allies, and private sector partners from maritime threats will be an interactive, layered structure of cooperating agencies and entities. MDA is a critical link to achieving this vision through timely delivery of required information resulting in decision superiority.

TABLE OF CONTENTS[2]

---

[2] Photos from cover page:

1. Icebreaker operations; image available at: http://www.uscg.mil/pacarea/cgcHealy/img/Healy_in_Ice.JPG. Accessed on 12 November 2013.

2. Port Operations, Los Angeles, California; image available at: http://www.sanpedro.com/sp_point/wrldptla.htm. Accessed on 12 November 2013.

3. Drug smuggling operations off the coast of Mexico; image available at: http://www.globalpost.com/dispatches/globalpost-blogs/que-pasa/mexico-drug-cartels-submarines-tanks-tunnels. Accessed on 12 November 2013.

I. CONTEXT

"As President, I have no greater responsibility than ensuring the safety and security of the United States and the American people. Meeting this responsibility requires the closest possible cooperation among our intelligence, military, diplomatic, homeland security, law enforcement, and public health communities, as well as with our partners at the State and local level and in the private sector. This cooperation, in turn, demands the timely and effective sharing of intelligence and information about threats to our Nation with those who need it, from the President to the police officer on the street."[3]

Maritime Domain Awareness (MDA) is the effective understanding of anything associated with the maritime domain that could impact the security, safety, economy, or environment of the United States.

The **Maritime Domain** is all areas and things of, on, under, relating to, adjacent to, or bordering on a sea, ocean, or other navigable waterway, including all maritime-related activities, infrastructure, people, cargo, vessels, and other conveyances.

Purpose

The *National Maritime Domain Awareness Plan* (NMDAP) supports Presidential Policy Directive 18 (PPD-18)[4] and the *National Strategy for Maritime Security* (NSMS)[5], and it strives to enhance ongoing MDA activities, such as ocean/waterway surveillance and maritime intelligence integration in support of MDA objectives. The Plan promotes global maritime security and prosperity through improved governance, policies, and actions that support the effective understanding of the maritime domain. Further, it encourages maritime stakeholders to identify and address MDA-related capability challenges and measure progress toward solutions. The Plan acknowledges initiatives to streamline the governance of MDA collaboration. Finally, the NMDAP serves to unify and support efforts to improve MDA and to promote secure and responsible information sharing to inform decision-making at all levels across the Global Maritime Community of Interest (GMCOI)[6].

This Plan is capable of responding to changed or improved capabilities, modifications to operational relationships, and updates to policy or strategy. A major aspect of this Plan – improving access to maritime information for all those with requisite needs and appropriate permissions – will be a challenging task.

---

[3]*National Strategy for Information Sharing and Safeguarding* (NSISS), at cover letter (December 2012).
[4]Presidential Policy Directive 18 (PPD-18): *Maritime Security* (August 14, 2012).
[5]*National Strategy for Maritime Security* (NSMS) (September 2005).
[6] This Plan supports the needs of the GMCOI, a common term used for the informal partnership that includes Federal departments and agencies, state, local, territorial, and tribal governments, industry, academia, and international partners. The GMCOI notionally includes all levels of government, domestic and international, along with private and commercial maritime stakeholders, because certain risks and interests are common to government, business, industry, and private citizens alike. Though informal, the GMCOI is bound by the common interest of maintaining the maritime domain for global security and prosperity.

Background

PPD-18 affirmed the NSMS, which included the *National Plan to Achieve Maritime Domain Awareness* (NPAMDA)[7] and the *Global Maritime Intelligence Integration* (GMII) Plan[8] as well as six other implementation plans to coordinate maritime security programs and initiatives across the GMCOI, and in particular, across departments and agencies of the U.S. Government. Although progress has been made toward goals set forth in the NPAMDA and GMII Plans, this bifurcation has proven to be less than optimal. The consolidation of the two plans into a single national MDA plan acknowledges advancements that have been made and highlights the inextricable relationship between MDA and maritime intelligence integration, promoting sustained progress while retaining a mandate for interagency action.

The NSMS continues to provide the strategic policy framework for implementing actions outlined in PPD-18. The NSMS calls for promoting unity of effort, fostering information sharing and integration, and facilitating the safe and efficient flow of commerce among government, public, and private entities. Since 2005, the GMCOI has enhanced transparency in the maritime domain through information sharing; enabled accurate and confident decisions across a full spectrum of threats and challenges; and sustained freedom of navigation, while promoting the legitimate, continuous, and efficient flow of commerce. Some notable examples include development and/or implementation of:

- Nationwide Automatic Identification System (NAIS);
- Maritime Safety and Security Information System (MSSIS);
- Long Range Identification and Tracking (LRIT);
- National Information Exchange Model (NIEM);
- Counter-Piracy Best Management Practices (BMP);
- Department of Transportation (DOT)/Maritime Administration (MARAD) Advisories;
- Single Integrated Lookout (SILO) list; and
- Geospatial Intelligence (GEOINT) Visualization Services (GVS).

Moving forward, MDA relies upon the continuous maturation of a collaborative environment of Federal, S/L/T/T, academic, industry, and international partners supporting the needs of the GMCOI. The NMDAP provides the goals, objectives, and framework for future implementation actions.

The Strategic Environment – The World As It Is

Covering more than 70 percent of the earth's surface, the maritime domain is a vital global resource, and its protection is a shared responsibility. The oceans, coasts, inland waterways, and Great Lakes provide jobs, food, energy resources, ecological services,

---

[7]*National Plan to Achieve Maritime Domain Awareness* (NPAMDA) (October 2005).
[8]*Global Maritime Intelligence Integration Plan* (GMII) (October 2005).

recreation, and tourism opportunities. This domain plays a critical supporting role in our Nation's transportation and trade, the global mobility of our Armed Forces, and the maintenance of international peace and security.[9]

The world's oceans and waterways enabled exploration of new lands by our ancestors, fueled the Industrial Revolution, and currently facilitate trade and provide sustenance and clean renewable energy for people across the globe.[10] These same oceans, along with our shorelines, waterways, ports, and infrastructure contiguous to our sea lines of communication offer opportunities and avenues for both man-made and natural threats that can harm our Nation's security and prosperity. Because 80 percent of the world's population lives within 200 miles of a shoreline, large numbers of people are also potentially subject to maritime-related threats.

The United States is a maritime nation, and the interconnectivity and stability of our national economy, commerce, and security is tied to the global maritime nature of international commerce. The maritime domain plays a critical role in the free flow of goods and services, as recognized in the *National Strategy for Global Supply Chain Security* (NSGSCS):

> International trade has been and continues to be a powerful engine of United States and global economic growth. In recent years, communications technology advances, and trade barrier and production cost reductions have contributed to global capital market expansion and new economic opportunity. The global supply chain system that supports this trade is essential to the United States' economy and is a critical global asset.[11]

As global markets leverage maritime-based commerce to sustain "just-in-time" logistics, decision-makers are faced with increasingly complex security issues. Massive amounts of layered and interrelated information exist because carriers and shippers use global intermodal connections to access hundreds of thousands of shippers, subcontractors, and producers. As a result, identifying potential threats within, or emanating from, the global supply chain has become more challenging due to difficulties in discerning illicit activity.

The maritime domain provides an expansive and extremely complex pathway for global commerce. It likewise presents a broad array of potential targets, the destruction or disruption of which would inflict significant harm, both physical and economic, on the United States and our partners.

> The deliberate misuse of the maritime domain to commit harmful, hostile, or unlawful acts, including those against the maritime transportation system, remains an enduring threat to the safety and security of the American people,

---

[9] Executive Order 13547: *Stewardship of the Ocean, Our Coasts, and the Great Lakes* (July 19, 2010).
[10] Supra note 7, p. 2.
[11]*National Strategy for Global Supply Chain Security* (NSGSCS), Executive Summary, p. 1 (January 2012).

to wider U.S. national security interests, and to the interests of our international allies and private sector partners.[12]

The NSMS defines the spectrum of maritime domain threats facing our Nation to include nation-states, terrorists, transnational criminal activities and piracy, environmental destruction, and illegal seaborne immigration. This spectrum of challenges involves and affects nearly every participant within the GMCOI. These challenges to our security and economic livelihood require a new mindset – one that views the totality of these threats and takes all necessary actions through an active, layered, shared defense. Additionally, the United States has an interest in working with our international partners to facilitate MDA and defend against the spectrum of maritime threats.

Those who threaten our security recognize the importance of the maritime domain as a potential medium for launching attacks and as an avenue for financial gain through the illicit movement of goods and human trafficking. The value of illicit trade around the globe in 2009 was estimated at $1.3 trillion, and the volume is increasing annually. Given that 90 percent of the world's legitimate commerce transits through the maritime domain, it is likely that the vast majority of the world's illicit traffic similarly touches the maritime environment.[13]

Finally, natural and man-made disasters present a risk of catastrophic and costly events. In addition to the potential for loss of life, such events present a threat of severe and adverse effects upon local, national, and regional economies and substantially affect the global supply chain. Enhanced MDA is vital to preparing, responding, and increasing resilience in the face of future catastrophes.

The Strategic Approach – The World We Seek

By addressing the maritime challenges our Nation and its partners currently face and promoting further progress in identifying and addressing MDA challenges, this Plan seeks to enable decision-makers by strengthening and enhancing the information sharing environment. We will accomplish this through the continued development of policies, enhanced situational awareness, intelligence integration, and information sharing and safeguarding capabilities to provide a maritime domain that supports prosperity and security within our domestic borders and around the world. Decision-makers at all levels require information that is available, discoverable, and accessible. In achieving this aim, we must protect current maritime information-sharing arrangements while simultaneously implementing effective measures to strengthen and significantly improve them through an MDA enterprise architecture. This will expedite the legitimate movement of goods

---

[12]Supra note 7, p. 2.

[13]*United Nations Office of Drugs & Crime, Action Against Transnational Organized Crime and Illicit Trafficking, Including Drug Trafficking,* Chapter 3 (2011-2013) available at:
http://www.unodc.org/documents/commissions/WG-GOVandFiN/Thematic_Programme_on_Organised_Crime_-_Final.pdf. Accessed on 12November2013.

and people in the maritime environment and provide countermeasures against those who seek to use the maritime domain to threaten our safety and security.

The world shares a collective interest in promoting the timely and efficient flow of legitimate commerce, while protecting and securing the maritime domain from exploitation and reducing its vulnerability to disruption by either man-made or natural disasters. We recognize security as an essential element of an efficient and functioning maritime domain. To successfully achieve these aims, an effective maritime awareness and information sharing arrangement must:

- **Improve detection, collection, and identification capabilities** that can be used to discover unknown or uncooperative maritime items of interest that represent threats, challenges, and opportunities to the GMCOI;
- **Recognize threats early** by effectively integrating intelligence, law enforcement information, and all source data from the public and private sectors throughout the GMCOI, according to established statutes and policy. Stakeholders can identify items of particular concern and seek to resolve or prepare as early as possible, thereby minimizing exposure, as well as maximizing response and resilience to, or recovery from, disruption or harm;
- **Enhance the protection of maritime infrastructure** by sharing and safeguarding relevant information to protect critical nodes and limiting access to those with validated permission and relevant roles and responsibilities; and,
- **Maximize legitimate use of the maritime domain** by modernizing maritime information sharing; safeguarding architecture, infrastructure, and processes to meet future validated requirements; and encouraging stakeholder collaboration.

It is United States policy to continue to use all instruments of national power and to coordinate wherever appropriate with S/L/T/T, academic, international, and private sector partners to strengthen maritime security, safeguard access, and promote the sustainable use of resources in the maritime domain.[14] Acknowledging that these challenges require interaction and cooperation with other nations, the *National Security Strategy* notes that collective action is the starting point for our strategic development.[15] MDA, and thus maritime security, is dependent on responsible information sharing and safeguarding by every level of government, our international partners, and private industry.

Effective measures to counter threats across the maritime domain rely upon information and threat sharing solutions that benefit stakeholder members. Maritime security is guided by an overarching philosophy that the GMCOI is best served through an enterprise architecture that provides individual members with secure, validated, and appropriate access to each other's data, while protecting personally identifiable information (PII), proprietary, and security information. This access should balance the need for information, security of that information, and appropriate access to the information, rather than simply using an organizational consolidation of information and

---

[14]Supra note 7, p.2.
[15]Ibid, p. 3.

intelligence activities.[16] This requires a comprehensive and robust layered approach consistent with the *National Strategy for Information Sharing and Safeguarding* (NSISS).

To provide the greatest benefit across the GMCOI, the Federal Government must expand and deepen collaborative relationships beyond virtual constructs to ensure the involvement of S/L/T/T authorities, academia, private industry, and our international partners. These partnerships, largely dependent upon common interests, are essential to achieving true MDA and thereby ensuring shared maritime security and global prosperity. Therefore, governance of maritime security issues under this Plan is designed to be collaborative and flexible by promoting forums for the exchange of MDA activities, information sharing and safeguarding, and outreach throughout the GMCOI to promote the collective good of national and global security and economic prosperity.

This Plan is intended to be enduring, evolving to inform and make the best use of changing capabilities, operational relationships, and policies and includes integrating maritime information for those with validated access throughout the GMCOI. The shared common awareness between the intelligence, law enforcement, and operational communities is complex and has many policy and legal implications that must be addressed to accomplish this necessary task.

Effective risk reduction in the maritime domain requires us to make faster and qualitatively better decisions based on awareness through the collection, integration, and timely dissemination of information to the consumers who require it to successfully perform their missions. An effective understanding of the global maritime domain enables national security, law enforcement, and civil emergency response actions; promotes safety and environmental stewardship; and supports strategic decision-making and operational threat response, while promoting freedom, protecting civil liberties, and providing greater opportunities for prosperity. Building upon the successes initiated by the NSMS and its subordinate plans, the NMDAP promotes decision superiority for tomorrow's maritime security through enhanced MDA.

---

[16] In this regard, this Plan is consistent with the mandate developed by the Director of National Intelligence in his 2012-2015 Strategic Plan, wherein the Office of the Director of National Intelligence seeks to improve "responsible and secure information sharing across the Intelligence Community and with external partners and customers," which is "imperative for effective collaboration, coordination, and intelligence integration."

II. PRIORITIES

Foundational Guidance

"Domain awareness requires integrating all-source intelligence, law enforcement information, and open-source data from the public and private sectors. It is heavily dependent on information sharing and requires unprecedented cooperation among the various elements of the public and private sectors, both nationally and internationally."[17]

Under the foundational guidance of PPD-18 and the NSMS, the NMDAP seeks to empower decision-makers to secure and promote the legitimate use of the maritime domain. This Plan promotes the integrated efforts of the GMCOI partners to:

- Prevent terrorist attacks and criminal, harmful, or hostile acts across the maritime domain by state and non-state actors;
- Protect population centers and critical infrastructure;
- Minimize damage to, and expedite recovery of, the maritime transportation system and related infrastructure in the wake of man-made or natural disasters;
- Maintain unimpeded access to global resources and markets; and
- Safeguard the oceans and their resources.[18]

To achieve this end-state, MDA efforts and activities must support the further development of improvements to situational awareness of the maritime domain. This, in turn, will create favorable conditions to enhance the following strategic priorities:

- Maximize maritime intelligence integration to support decision-making;
- Maximize appropriate availability of relevant maritime intelligence and information;
- Enhance international and industry partnerships, cooperation, and information sharing and safeguarding;
- Improve GMCOI-assured access to maritime related threat information; and,
- Integrate MDA with land, air, cyberspace, and space domains to achieve integrated domain awareness.

We strive to position GMCOI leaders at all levels to better prepare for, prevent, mitigate, respond to, and recover from maritime related threats. Enhancing MDA, including information sharing and safeguarding, will further promote the security and stability of the maritime domain, including population centers and maritime-related intermodal infrastructure.

While this Plan responds to its foundational strategic guidance, it also aligns with other national strategies and policies that have relevance to the maritime domain, including the

---

[17] Supra note 8, p. 16

[18] Ibid., p. 8; Supra note 7, p. 4

NSISS, the NSGSCS, the *National Ocean Policy*,[19] the *National Strategy for the Arctic Region*, and emerging national-level policy.

MDA must also inform those entities with maritime equities of these strategic priorities to help them prevent catastrophic loss of life and manage cascading, disruptive effects on the U.S. and global economies across multiple threat scenarios.[20] A unified effort is enhanced through national strategies and plans, which balance resiliency with risk-informed prevention, protection, and preparation activities to manage the most serious risks to critical infrastructure[21] and key resources[22] (CIKR) associated with the maritime domain.[23]

With so much of the Nation's and the world's commerce flowing through the maritime domain and its related infrastructure, enhanced MDA continues to be vital in supporting leaders and decision-makers to successfully perform their missions. To undertake this endeavor, we must identify and remedy policy, resourcing, and information sharing barriers that traditional hierarchical organizational structures encourage and that prevent closing or mitigating identified MDA challenges.

MDA Core Principles

Promote Unity of Effort. MDA requires a coordinated effort across the GMCOI, including public and private sector organizations, and international partners. Maritime security benefits all and is enhanced through the increased participation of maritime stakeholders.

Foster Information Sharing and Safeguarding. MDA depends on secure, effective information sharing and safeguarding with partners possessing validated access. To advance global MDA, we seek to appropriately leverage existing, and develop new bilateral or multilateral information sharing agreements, arrangements, and/or international conventions and treaties. For example, this type of exchange could include collaboration with industry and international cooperation on the commercial use of space for MDA[24] to benefit the GMCOI.

---

[19]National Ocean Policy - Executive Order 13547, *Stewardship of the Ocean, Our Coasts, and the Great Lakes* (July 19, 2010).

[20] Presidential Policy Directive 21 (PPD-21): *Critical Infrastructure Security and Resilience* (February 12, 2013).

[21]The term "critical infrastructure" means systems and assets, whether physical or virtual, so vital to the United States that the incapacity or destruction of such systems and assets would have a debilitating impact on security, national economic security, national public health or safety, or any combination of those matters. 42 U.S.C. §5195c(e).

[22]The Homeland Security Act of 2002, 6 U.S.C. §101(10).

[23]*National Infrastructure Protection Plan* (NIPP): *Partnering to Enhance Protection and Resiliency*, at Preface (2009).

[24] Presidential Policy Directive 4 (PPD-4): *National Space Policy* (June 29, 2010).

Facilitate Safe and Efficient Flow of Legitimate Commerce. Maritime and economic security is mutually reinforcing. All GMCOI members must recognize that the safe and efficient flow of commerce is enhanced and harmonized by an effective, shared understanding of the maritime domain.

MDA Goals

The purpose of MDA is to **facilitate timely, accurate, and informed decision-making**. Decision-makers require timely, accurate, and relevant information to successfully prepare for, prevent, respond to, and recover from threats. MDA addresses core safety, security, economic, and environmental priorities and allows us to better respond to maritime threats and challenges. MDA does not direct actions but enables decision-makers to take action more quickly and with greater precision.

MDA includes the ability to monitor activities in such a way that trends and anomalies can be identified early to facilitate decision-makers' responses. Data alone is insufficient; information must be collected, fused, analyzed, protected, and disseminated so that decision-makers are able to anticipate potential threats and take effective and appropriate action. In simplifying today's complex and ambiguous security environment, MDA seeks to achieve the following goals:

- Enhance transparency in the maritime domain to detect, deter, and defeat threats as early as possible;
- Enable accurate, dynamic, and confident decisions and responses to the full spectrum of maritime threats and challenges through information sharing and safeguarding;
- Further partnerships to promote and facilitate maritime domain information sharing, safeguarding, capacity building, and integration; and
- Preserve our Nation's rights, freedoms of navigation and over-flight, and uses of the sea and airspace recognized under international law while promoting the lawful, continuous, and efficient flow of commerce.

Achieving these goals will make MDA the critical enabler for national maritime security and promote effective decision-making for timely maritime response.

MDA Objectives

This Plan builds upon past success in promoting maritime security, MDA, and maritime intelligence integration. It seeks to further enhance the effective understanding of the maritime domain by leveraging and improving our ability to share and safeguard maritime information to create more favorable conditions for global maritime security and prosperity. Therefore, this Plan coordinates MDA policies and activities across the Federal Government and encourages the involvement of the GMCOI.

MDA requires the successful development, integration, and implementation of policies, processes, standards, and technologies to promote secure and responsible sharing and safeguarding of maritime information.[25] For these reasons, this Plan envisions four primary objectives to achieve the aforementioned goals:

- **Organize stakeholders through governance**. Proper governance to coordinate Federal maritime stakeholder activities will promote an interagency shared perspective, which will acknowledge and balance the equities of Federal, S/L/T/T, academic, private sector, and international maritime stakeholders;

- **Continue to mitigate MDA challenges.** This Plan acknowledges previous work to identify MDA challenges, promotes the development of metrics to determine when a challenge has been addressed or mitigated, and identifies the tools to address those challenges. The Plan also recognizes that new and emerging challenges continue to present themselves, validating the requirement for a continuous reassessment process using risk management methodologies;

- **Improve Domain Awareness through enterprise-level access to data.** This Plan promotes maritime information sharing by transitioning from organization-centric databases to web-centric enterprise services that retrieve data from multiple sources (e.g. clouds, databases). This shift provides authorized users with more flexible access to a greater number of sources, types, and volume of data and the ability to search databases without relying on point-to-point access. Data, under this construct, should be authoritative and conform to recognized standards, such as those currently employed under the National Information Exchange Model (NIEM); and

- **Enhance collaboration through outreach.** This Plan encourages broad interaction to identify organizations, partnerships, best practices, and other efforts that enhance maritime security through expanded MDA collaboration between the GMCOI members. By collaborating on MDA initiatives and incorporating Federal, S/L/T/T, academic, private, and international maritime partners, this Plan will support and improve interagency capabilities to effectively share and safeguard information on people, cargo, vessels, infrastructure, natural and man-made disasters, and other potential threats within the maritime domain.

Maritime Intelligence Integration

Underpinning our ability to understand the maritime domain, determine potential threats, and enhance effective decision-making is our ability to integrate maritime intelligence. A coordinated and synchronized intelligence enterprise is a priority for effective security efforts across the maritime domain. To maximize MDA, the United States must leverage and integrate the diverse expertise of the intelligence and law enforcement communities for a global maritime intelligence capability, according to established statutes and policy.

---

[25] Supra note 6, p. 1.

Crucial opportunities to prevent an incident or provide an early response can be lost without effective awareness of activities within the maritime domain. Awareness grants time and distance to detect, deter, interdict, and overcome threats.[26]

The Director of National Intelligence (DNI) designated the National Maritime Intelligence-Integration Office (NMIO) to coordinate and facilitate maritime intelligence integration and information sharing in support of MDA. NMIO facilitates a unified maritime perspective by coordinating with the Intelligence Community (IC) and across the GMCOI to advance maritime intelligence sharing and integration for early threat detection and decision superiority.

It has been stated that, "Intelligence Integration is the Intelligence Community's unity of effort to produce the best intelligence possible."[27] Advancing maritime intelligence integration relies heavily upon effective collaboration among the members of the IC. The IC supports the strategic objectives of this Plan by:

- Timely collection, analysis, production, dissemination, and sharing of all maritime intelligence and information regarding potential threats to U.S. and partner interests;[28]
- Identifying and integrating new or existing information and data sources in the shared information environment of the IC regarding potential threats to maritime security;[29]
- Resolving MDA challenges, as noted in Appendix C, associated with maritime intelligence activities involving collections, analysis, and dissemination;
- Ensuring related intelligence reports and products are drafted for widest dissemination possible;[30] and
- Recognizing linkages that require collaboration across all domains, such as in the global supply chain, where the maritime domain is inextricably linked with the air, land, space, and cyberspace domains to detect, deter, and defeat threats.[31]

---

[26] Supra note 6, p. 9.

[27] Robert Cardillo, "The Challenge and Promise of Intelligence Integration," *Studies in Intelligence Vol. 56, No. 2* (June 2012).

[28] IC Directive 902, "Global Maritime and Air Intelligence Integration," pg. 3 (January 2009).

[29] Ibid.

[30]Widest dissemination relies upon IC members employing concepts identified in IC Directive 208, *Write for Maximum Utility*, (December 2008) and IC Directive 209, *Tearline Production and Dissemination* (September 2012).

[31] Supra note 14, p. 2, footnote 2.

III. Implementation Plan

"To effectively craft and implement a sustainable, results-oriented national security strategy, there must be effective cooperation between the branches of government."[32]

The NMDAP recognizes the need for reliable information to evaluate threats and challenges, assess risks, and ensure our ability to appropriately share vital information.

This Plan seeks to ensure that the Nation and its partners have the appropriate MDA systems, procedures, and relationships to support prudent decision-making that accounts for the seriousness and likelihood of threats and challenges confronting the GMCOI. In this way, we best position decision-makers at every level of government and within the private sector to identify, prepare for, prevent, mitigate, respond to, and recover from the harm those threats and challenges present. Appendix A describes the primary MDA information categories necessary to support decision-makers confronting threats in the maritime domain.

The way forward requires a sustained effort to establish and maintain information sharing partnerships within the U.S. Government and with government and law enforcement at every level, along with our foreign partners, private industry, and academia. Over the next five years, this Plan will guide Federal departments, agencies, and their components to implement activities that address the MDA objectives:

- Organize stakeholders through governance;
- Continue to mitigate MDA challenges;
- Improve domain awareness through enterprise-level access to data; and,
- Enhance collaboration through outreach.

MDA must support, and be supported by, an assessment process that ensures information requirements across the GMCOI are addressed. To that end, the Departments of Defense (DoD), Transportation (DOT), and Homeland Security (DHS) will work together along with other interested Federal departments and agencies, including law enforcement and the Intelligence Community (IC), to fully identify those information requirements through a risk assessment process. That process must pertain not only to security, but also to commerce and economic stability as well as environmental protection and sustainment.

Ultimately, MDA is recognized as a component of several interconnected domains, including maritime, land, air, space, and cyberspace. As we gain greater awareness of each domain, we must simultaneously seek ways to identify their interaction and understand how they affect each other. An integrated domain approach will enhance our situational awareness and promote greater communication while simultaneously denying access to and use of these domains by those who seek to threaten our way of life.

---

[32] Supra note 19, p. 51.

Organize Stakeholders Through Governance

Based upon the progress made to mitigate threats identified by MDA challenge assessments, the MDA ESC will continue to resolve or mitigate these challenges by using them as a starting point in a risk assessment process. The MDA ESC will continue to develop metrics to identify when a challenge is addressed or mitigated and promote collaboration between Federal MDA activities. Recognizing that additional challenges will continue to present themselves, the MDA ESC will promote the identification of new or emerging challenges, as required, and develop a continuous reassessment process.

National Security Staff (NSS)/Maritime Security Interagency Policy Committee (MSIPC) or its successor

The NSS/MSIPC was established to act as the primary forum for interagency coordination and implementation of maritime security policies, strategies, and initiatives.

The MSIPC, supported by its Maritime Security Working Group (MSWG), guides the development of NSMS supporting plans. The governance provided in this Plan aligns under the authority of PPD-1 and PPD-18.

MDA Executive Steering Committee (ESC)

The MDA ESC is comprised of senior executive-level Principals designated by their respective departmental Executive Agents (EA) for MDA from cabinet-level departments (currently DoD, DOT, and DHS) and the designated maritime representative of the IC. The MDA ESC coordinates MDA policies, strategies, and initiatives. MDA ESC membership may change upon the consensus of the MDA ESC principals. The MDA ESC also provides forums, activities, and venues to engage the GMCOI to promote collaboration and information sharing to enhance MDA. See Appendix B for further information.

Continue to Mitigate MDA Challenges

In June 2010, the MDA ESC identified interagency MDA gaps relating to the maritime domain (Appendix C). This effort leveraged the work and results of previous MDA analyses and studies under the authority of the NSMS and its subordinate plans. In so doing, the MDA ESC reduced duplication of effort among the various agencies and provided alignment among offices and missions, while focusing on implementing solutions. The MDA ESC will continue to address challenges, evaluate risk, and promote the appropriate solutions to meet this objective.

This effort identified problems common to many GMCOI members. In response, the MDA ESC has begun to advance relevant solutions across the broad interagency community. This initiative to enhance MDA exemplified the effectiveness of developing national security solutions through interagency collaboration, using a whole-of-government approach.

Based upon the progress made to mitigate threats identified by MDA challenge assessments, the MDA ESC will continue to resolve or mitigate these challenges by using them as a starting point in a risk assessment process. The MDA ESC will continue to develop metrics to identify when a challenge is addressed or mitigated and promote collaboration between Federal MDA activities. Recognizing that additional challenges will continue to present themselves, the MDA ESC will promote the identification of new or emerging challenges, as required, and develop a continuous reassessment process.

Improve Domain Awareness Through Enterprise-Level Access to Data

Information is a national asset and, as such, requires a responsible balancing act between information sharing and safeguarding.[33] The Information Sharing Environment is comprised of and operated by partners across all levels of the Federal government, S/L/T/T, academia, the private sector, and international partners. Each GMCOI member has a need to collaborate, share, and safeguard information relevant to their objectives. In accordance with Federal law, information sharing must protect private sector proprietary and PPI from unauthorized access and misuse. Consistent with the NSISS, this implementation Plan promotes the development of the national maritime information sharing environment to support MDA.

The MDA ESC will lead the Federal interagency maritime stakeholders in collaboration to establish a national-level MDA enterprise architecture which may include:

- Enterprise, web-centric, cloud-based, information and services;
- Common data standards; and,
- Data access policy.

The transition to national-level collaboration through an information sharing environment that enables data access through multiple sources (e.g. clouds or databases) provides authorized users with more flexible access to a greater number of sources, types, and volume of data and the ability to search databases without relying on point-to-point access. Under this construct data should be authoritative and conform to recognized standards, such as those currently employed under the NIEM.

Enhance Collaboration Through Outreach

Due to the diverse equities of the GMCOI, recognizing and understanding the concerns and priorities of each member presents many challenges. The MDA ESC will encourage information exchange to identify stakeholder efforts where alignment and unity of effort would prove beneficial. Through forums for discussion, the MDA ESC will expand existing partnerships to exchange MDA information in support of common initiatives. Where possible, enterprise applications and successful projects already moving forward

---

[33] Supra note 6, p. 6.

will be leveraged to enable broader participation of the GMCOI. The MDA ESC will link GMCOI members together to consolidate efforts and expand understanding among relevant Federal, S/L/T/T, industry, academic, and international stakeholders. This Plan acknowledges the value of coordination with international partners and encourages cooperation to address threats to national security.

IV. Conclusion

The United States and its GMCOI partners continue to face a complex environment in the maritime domain. In the 21st century, risk results from a complex mix of man-made and naturally occurring threats and hazards including terrorist attacks, accidents, natural disasters, and other emergencies. Within the maritime context, critical infrastructure related to our security and economic vitality may be directly exposed to harm by events themselves or indirectly exposed as a result of the dependencies and interdependencies among related resources.[34] Challenges in the maritime domain will continue to be serious and complex. These challenges to our security and economic livelihood require a whole-of-government and whole-of-community GMCOI approach that recognizes the total threat and takes all necessary actions through active, layered, and shared defense.

To achieve this goal, the Nation must strengthen the means to detect and deter illegal or harmful activity designed to take advantage of inherent vulnerabilities within the maritime domain. To protect, prevent, mitigate, and enhance recovery from such threats, we must achieve a more comprehensive and effective understanding of the maritime domain.

Intergovernmental organizations must work closely with departments and agencies responsible for developing and implementing plans. Over the long-term, it is imperative that the efforts and activities among various Federal and S/L/T/T stakeholders as well as those of our international, academic, and private sector partners are complementary, easily integrated, and provide the effective capabilities required to identify, share, and safeguard information regarding maritime threats.

MDA is a critical enabler that allows leaders at all levels to make effective decisions and act as early as possible against a vast array of threats and challenges for the security and prosperity of the United States, its allies, and partners.

The implementation of this Plan will necessarily be adaptive and continuous. The NMDAP sets forth the path toward achieving understanding of the maritime domain and increasing our effectiveness in meeting global security and economic requirements. Achieving the capabilities called for in this Plan requires the continued investment of our collective resources: intellectual, technological, and human within the entire GMCOI.

---

[34] Supra note 29, at Preface

APPENDIX A: MDA INFORMATION CATEGORIES

The global maritime domain includes a broad array of inter-related and connected functions operating within, adjacent to, and beyond the physical oceans and waterways. To detect and interdict threats within an environment that crosses domestic and international jurisdictions requires a current and updated level of awareness that must be better synthesized and shared.

MDA requires information involving a broad range of data categories which may include:

- **Vessels**—information such as flag, type, classification society, tonnage, maximum speed, origin, positional information, next port of call, last port of call, track history, construction and outfitting, history (build, employment, and regulatory), documentation, acoustics, capacities, etc.
- **Cargo**—information derived from cargo manifests and bills of lading, including characteristics, origin, handling instructions, destination, and hazard class, as well as information derived from customs and hazardous material inspections; chemical, biological, nuclear, radiation, or explosive detection sensors; and data exchange and mandatory reporting systems.
- **People and Organizations**—information regarding vessel owners and charterers, crew and passengers, freight forwarders, husbanding agents, insurers, lien holders, port terminal operators, stevedores, etc., as well as financial transactions that people and organizations may be involved in that indicate whether relationships are legitimate, illicit, or demonstrative of overt or covert activity.
- **Infrastructure**—information with maritime attributes, including requisite geospatial information, such as the following:
  - Ports, Waterways, and Facilities - piers, terminals, cranes, fueling facilities, and other resources or key limits, such as vessel traffic services and vessel separation schemes, shipping and great circle routes, international maritime boundaries, disposal sites, offshore leasing sites (e.g., oil fields, wind farms, and other national energy security components), etc.
  - Critical Infrastructure - locks, bridges, tunnels, channels, aids to navigation, undersea cables, pipelines, nuclear and other power plants, and intermodal connections.
- **Environment**—information, data, and metadata on weather, including wind, sea, swell, tides and currents, other hydrographic and bathymetric data, sea temperature and salinity, and ice flows, as well as information regarding maritime natural resources, regulated fisheries, migratory patterns, marine sanctuaries, marine protected areas and species, pollution, emission control areas, and impacts from offshore energy development, etc.

Because of the maritime domain's complexity and expanse, the potential for exploitation of vulnerabilities for unlawful purposes makes information and intelligence collection on vessels, cargo, and people the most critical of the above categories, although awareness of related maritime infrastructure and the marine environment are critically important for engaging in operational maritime activities.

APPENDIX B: ORGANIZATIONS

Department of Commerce (DOC). A United States Federal cabinet-level agency of the Executive Branch that promotes international trade, economic growth, and technological advancement. It performs many activities related to business, trade, and technology.

Department of Defense (DoD). A United States Federal cabinet-level agency established under the National Security Act of 1947, responsible for providing the military forces needed to deter war and protect the security of the United States. The major elements of these forces are the Army, Navy, Air Force, and Marine Corps. The President is the Commander-in-Chief, while the Secretary of Defense exercises authority, direction, and control over the Department. This organizational structure includes the Office of the Secretary of Defense, Organization of the Chairman of the Joint Chiefs of Staff, the 3 Military Departments, the Combatant Commands, the Office of the Inspector General, 18 Defense Agencies, 10 DoD Field Activities, and other organizations.

Department of Homeland Security (DHS). A United States Federal cabinet-level agency created under the Homeland Security Act of 2002 to plan, lead, and coordinate Federal government activities related to homeland security, including intelligence, critical infrastructure protection, customs, border security, transportation and supply chain security, emergency preparedness and response, and science and technology.

Department of State (DOS). Often referred to as the U.S. State Department, DOS is the U.S. Federal cabinet-level department responsible for international relations of the United States, equivalent to the Foreign Ministry in other countries. The State Department is also responsible for formulation, coordination, and oversight of foreign policy related to international communications and information policy.

Department of Transportation (DOT). A United States Federal cabinet-level agency established by Congress on October 15, 1966. Under Title 49, U.S. Code, §101 et seq., its mission is to achieve the national objectives of general welfare, economic growth and stability, and security of the United States that require the development of transportation policies and programs that contribute to providing fast, safe, efficient, and convenient transportation at the lowest cost consistent with those and other national objectives, including the efficient use and conservation of the resources of the United States.

Global Maritime Operational Threat Response (MOTR) Coordination Center (GMCC). The GMCC is a DHS entity that provides a capability to coordinate interagency response to maritime threats involving U.S. interests worldwide, pursuant to the MOTR Plan and MSIPC-approved MOTR protocols.[35] During MOTR coordination activities, the GMCC is accountable to the NSS.

---

[35]Presidential Policy Directive 18 /PPD-18: *Maritime Security*, Supra note 1, p. 5 (August 14, 2012)

The U.S. Intelligence Community (IC).[36] The U.S. IC is a coalition of 17 agencies and organizations within the executive branch that work independently and collaboratively to gather the intelligence necessary to conduct foreign relations and national security activities.

International Partners. Ensuring the security of the maritime domain is inherently an international effort requiring a global maritime information sharing enterprise that supports the intelligence and information needs of the GMCOI. Under the NSMS, DOS is the lead Federal agency for international outreach. As such, the MDA ESC will coordinate international MDA outreach efforts with DOS to ensure unity of effort. NMIO, in coordination with Office of the Director of National Intelligence (ODNI), will lead maritime-related IC engagements with foreign partners and international organizations to ensure that activities are aligned and synchronized, as well as to facilitate partnership development.

Maritime Security Interagency Policy Committee (MSIPC). The National Security Staff (NSS) MSIPC, or its successor, consists of senior executives and flag officers responsible for maritime policy, operations, and intelligence throughout the Federal Government. The MSIPC reviews maritime policy and provides guidance for strategic maritime issues. PPD-1 defines the role of Federal interagency policy committees. The NSS Senior Director of the MSIPC may also establish interagency working groups, such as the Maritime Security Working Group (MSWG), consisting of action officers from MSIPC member organizations, to coordinate and work specific issues.

Maritime Domain Awareness Executive Steering Committee (MDA ESC). The MDA ESC coordinates MDA policies, strategies, and initiatives. It is comprised of senior executive-level principals designated by their respective departmental EA for MDA from cabinet-level departments (currently DoD, DOT, and DHS) and NMIO, as the designated representative of the IC. MDA ESC membership may change upon the consensus of the MDA ESC Principals. Federal departments with maritime stakeholder interests are encouraged to designate a departmental EA for MDA and provide a senior executive-level representative to participate in the MDA ESC forums.

The MDA ESC meets routinely and, under this Plan, is responsible to the NSS MSIPC, in accordance with PPD-1 and PPD-18, to oversee and coordinate interagency collaboration on MDA policy and activities to promote maritime domain information sharing, prioritize MDA efforts, develop MDA work plans, and close or mitigate recognized national-level MDA challenges. The MDA ESC principals will leverage their respective partnerships with industry, academia, S/L/T/T governments, and international partners to reach out to and better position the GMCOI to achieve collective MDA goals. The MDA ESC will also provide forums, activities, and venues to engage the GMCOI to promote collaboration and information sharing to ultimately enhance MDA.

---

[36]Supra note 32.

The MDA ESC may create working groups as required to promote the interagency coordination of proposed policies and activities that will potentially affect the maritime domain and the members of the GMCOI. The Chair of the MDA ESC represents the positions of the MDA EAs at external meetings, such as before the MSIPC. Currently, Director, NMIO is Chair of the MDA ESC and, as such, provides staff for executive secretariat support to this forum and is the requisite impartial voice for national-level maritime related issues to the NSS/MSIPC and other interagency policy committees.

National Maritime Interagency Advisory Group (NIAG). To support the whole-of-government information sharing needs of the GMCOI, this forum specifically advises the Chair of the MDA ESC to:

- Collaborate to identify national maritime-related issues[37] and requirements, including those from national, international, academic, and private sector organizations;
- Inform, lead, advocate, and reach out to all aspects of the GMCOI; and,
- Ensure the GMCOI's maritime information and analysis needs are effectively represented.

The NIAG is a federally-sponsored, whole-of-government forum and includes representatives from the Federal interagency, the IC, and law enforcement, and participants from private industry, academia, and international partners. With input from these GMCOI members and other participants, the NIAG advises the Chair of the MDA ESC on maritime information needs and concerns.

National Maritime Intelligence-Integration Office (NMIO). NMIO was established by the DNI to coordinate maritime intelligence integration and information sharing and advance national-level MDA. NMIO[38] facilitates a unified maritime perspective by coordinating with the IC and across the GMCOI to advance maritime intelligence sharing and integration for decision superiority. NMIO receives oversight and strategic direction from ODNI and administrative support from the Department of the Navy. NMIO facilitates IC support to the strategic actions according to this Plan.

National Oceanic and Atmospheric Administration (NOAA). A United States Federal agency within the DOC, it is a scientific agency that focuses on the conditions of the oceans and the atmosphere. NOAA seeks to expand understanding and predict changes in climate, weather, oceans, and coasts, as well as to conserve and manage coastal and marine ecosystems and resources.

Office of the Director of National Intelligence (ODNI). A United States Federal cabinet-level agency established by Congress through the Intelligence Reform and Terrorism Prevention Act of 2004 (IRTPA), effecting major amendments to the National

---

[37] National maritime-related issues include the broad environment of maritime security, MDA, maritime intelligence integration, and maritime transportation system preparedness and resiliency.
[38] Supra note 7, p. 5.

Security Act of 1947. The President signed IRTPA into law on 17 December 2004; ODNI began operations following the appointment of the first DNI in February 2005.

Private, Commercial Partners. Private industry possesses invaluable insight to implement national strategies and supporting plans. The interagency must integrate intelligence and information sharing holistically. MARAD, as the DOT MDA EA, is the lead advocate with regards to outreach and information sharing with the maritime industry and private sector. The MDA ESC, in particular DOT, DHS, and NMIO, will encourage the private sector to work with fusion centers, maritime advocacy groups/organizations, and DHS infrastructure protection programs to promote maritime and economic security through partnerships and information sharing.

Program Manager – Information Sharing Environment (PM-ISE). Established by Congress through the IRTPA, PM-ISE's mission is to advance responsible information sharing to further counter-terrorism and homeland security, improve nationwide decision-making by transforming information ownership to stewardship, and promote partnerships across Federal, S/L/T/T governments, the private sector, and international partners. Due to its national role in information sharing and safeguarding, PM-ISE is a stakeholder and partner with the MDA ESC, Federal maritime stakeholders, and the broader GMCOI to promote information sharing to protect against man-made and natural maritime threats.

State, Local, Tribal, Territorial (S/L/T/T) Partners. S/L/T/T partners are both customers and contributors of information and situational awareness, law enforcement information, and intelligence. A primary interface for maritime information exchange with S/L/T/T partners will be their fusion centers and respective port and maritime agencies. Engagement with indigenous communities, particularly in remote areas, is critical in gathering information related to MDA and national security. NMIO will work with DHS and the DHS MDA EA to advocate information sharing for maritime security, MDA, and intelligence integration. NMIO will work with DHS, S/L/T/T fusion centers, port authorities, and respective maritime agencies to promote and establish pathways for maritime information exchange.

APPENDIX C: MDA CHALLENGES

In June 2010, the MDA ESC initiated an interagency effort to identify and address gaps relating to the maritime domain. This effort leveraged the work and results of previous MDA analyses and studies under the authority of the NSMS and its subordinate plans. By pursuing an interagency path, the MDA ESC successfully reduced duplication of effort among the various agencies and provided alignment among agencies and missions while focusing on implementing solutions.[39] The MDA ESC will continue to address challenges, evaluate risk, and promote appropriate solutions to meet this objective.

This effort identified opportunities for improvement common to many GMCOI members; in response, the MDA ESC sought to advance relevant solutions across the broad community. This initiative to enhance MDA exemplified the effectiveness of developing national security solutions through interagency collaboration, using a whole-of-government approach. See Table 1.

Challenge #	U.S. MDA Challenge Title
1	Collection for Non-Emitting and Uncooperative Vessels
2	Fusion and Analysis for Non-Emitting and Uncooperative Vessels
3	National MDA Enterprise Assessment
4	Understanding Maritime Activity
5	Determination of Anomalous Behavior
6	National MDA Strategy Development
7	Maritime Personnel Security Information
8	Shared Situational Analysis Capability
9	Fusion and Analysis for Cargo Data
10	MDA Information Collection Requirements Definition and Planning
11	Collection for Cargo Transiting Internationally
12	Fusion and Analysis for Maritime Personnel
13	Vessel Identification and Tracking
14	Domestic Sensor Supply and Deployment Shortfall
15	End-to-End Connectivity for the MDA Community
16	MDA Collaborative Tools Development
17	Enterprise Alignment of the National MDA Effort
18	MDA Network Management Services
19	MDA Information Assurance and Security Procedures
20	Non-Standard Collection on Safety of Life at Sea (SOLAS) Vessels

TABLE 1. U.S. MDA CHALLENGES

---

[39]*Maritime Domain Awareness Interagency Solutions Analysis Current State Report* (CSR) (June 2010)

APPENDIX D: TERMS AND ACRONYMS

TERMS

Critical Infrastructure. Systems and assets, whether physical or virtual, so vital to the United States that the incapacity or destruction of such systems and assets would have a debilitating impact on security, national economic security, national public health or safety, or any combination of those matters. 42 U.S.C. §5195c(e).

Decision Superiority. Better decisions arrived at and implemented faster than an opponent can react, or in a noncombat situation, at a tempo that allows the force to shape the situation or react to changes and accomplish its mission. Decision superiority does not automatically result from informational superiority. Organizational and doctrinal adaptation, relevant training and experience, and the proper command and control mechanisms and tools are equally necessary. Chairman of the Joint Chiefs of Staff (CJCS), *Joint Vision 2020* (Pentagon, Washington D.C., U.S. Government Printing Office, June 2000), pg. 11-12.

Global Maritime Community of Interest (GMCOI). The GMCOI is a common term used for the informal partnership that includes Federal departments and agencies, S/L/T/T governments, industry, academia, and international partners. The GMCOI notionally includes all levels of government, domestic and international, along with private and commercial maritime stakeholders, because certain risks and interests are common to government, business, industry, and private citizens alike. Though informal, the GMCOI is bound by the common interest of maintaining the maritime domain for global security and prosperity.

Global Supply Chain. A system of organizations, people, technologies, activities, information, and resources involved in moving products or services from suppliers to customers around the world. Supply chain activities transform natural resources, raw materials, and components into finished products delivered to the end customers. The global system relies upon an interconnected web of transportation infrastructure and pathways, information technology, and cyber and energy networks.

Intelligence. The product resulting from the collection, processing, integration, evaluation, analysis, and interpretation of available information concerning foreign nations, hostile or potentially hostile forces or elements, or areas of actual or potential operations. The term is also applied to the activity which results in the product and to the organizations engaged in such activity (*Joint Publication 2-0*, Joint Intelligence, 22 June 2007, pg. GL-11).

Intelligence Integration. The synchronization of the IC to achieve unity of effort in a particular issue of interest. At an operational level, it is the synchronization of collection and analytic efforts to achieve a unified strategy and approach to an issue.

Key Resources. Publicly or privately controlled resources essential to the minimal operations of the economy and government. The Homeland Security Act of 2002; 6 U.S.C. §101(10).

Maritime Domain. The maritime domain is all areas and things of, on, under, relating to, adjacent to, or bordering on a sea, ocean, or other navigable waterway, including all maritime related activities, infrastructure, people, cargo, vessels, and other conveyances.

Maritime Domain Awareness (MDA). MDA is the effective understanding of anything associated with the maritime domain that could impact the security, safety, economy, or environment of the United States.

MDA and Maritime Intelligence Integration. MDA and maritime intelligence integration are ultimately the responsibility of the various Federal departments and agencies that comprise the MSIPC or its successor. This Plan's governance and coordination structure reinforces and supports their respective primacy and authority, while promoting interagency efforts of this Plan consistent with PPD-1 and PPD-18. Information, as used in this document, includes everything from all-source data to finished intelligence assessments.

Maritime Operational Threat Response (MOTR) Plan. MOTR is the presidentially-approved plan to achieve a coordinated U.S. Government response to threats against the United States and its interests in the maritime domain. The MOTR Plan establishes a process for initiating real-time Federal interagency communication, coordination, and decision-making through an integrated network of command centers.

National Infrastructure Protection Plan (NIPP). The product of a DHS-led process that involves representatives of all levels of Government as well as critical infrastructure owners and operators across all 16 sectors. The goals of the plan are to:

- Assess and analyze threats to, vulnerabilities of, and consequences to critical infrastructure to inform risk management activities;
- Secure critical infrastructure against human, physical, and cyber threats through sustainable efforts to reduce risk, while accounting for the costs and benefits of security investments;
- Enhance critical infrastructure resilience by minimizing the adverse consequences of incidents through advance planning and mitigation efforts, as well as effective responses to save lives and ensure the rapid recovery of essential services;
- Share actionable and relevant information across the critical infrastructure community to build awareness and enable risk-informed decision making; and
- Promote learning and adaptation during and after exercises and incidents related to security and resilience.

National Strategy for Maritime Security (NSMS). A comprehensive national strategy requiring the Federal government, and in particular, the Secretaries of the DoD and DHS, to better integrate and synchronize their existing department-level strategies related to maritime security, to ensure their effective and efficient implementation. DoD and DHS, in coordination with other interested agencies, developed supporting plans to address the specific threats and challenges of and in the maritime environment, each addressing different aspects of maritime security. The supporting Plans are intended to mutually reinforce each other. The supporting plans originally included:

- *National Plan to Achieve Maritime Domain Awareness*;
- *Global Maritime Intelligence Integration Plan*;
- *Maritime Operational Threat Response Plan*;
- *International Outreach and Coordination Strategy*;
- *Maritime Infrastructure Recovery Plan*;
- *Maritime Transportation System Security Plan*;
- *Maritime Commerce Security Plan*; and
- *Domestic Outreach Plan*.

Since the original efforts to develop the NSMS, efforts have been conducted to streamline this supporting plan system, resulting in the consolidation of the *National Plan to Achieve Maritime Domain Awareness* with the *Global Maritime Intelligence Integration Plan* to create the *National Maritime Domain Awareness Plan*, thereby reducing the number of active plans.

Security. A condition that results from the establishment and maintenance of protective measures to ensure a state of inviolability from hostile acts or influences. (Joint Publication 3-10).

ACRONYMS

BMP	Best Management Practices
CIKR	Critical Infrastructure and Key Resources
DHS	Department of Homeland Security
DOC	Department of Commerce
DoD	Department of Defense
DOJ	Department of Justice
DOS	Department of State
DOT	Department of Transportation
DNI	Director of National Intelligence
EA	Executive Agent
ESC	Executive Steering Committee
GEOINT	Geospatial Intelligence
GMCC	Global MOTR Coordination Center
GMCOI	Global Maritime Community of Interest
GMII	Global Maritime Intelligence Integration (Plan)
GVS	GEOINT Visualization Services
IC	U.S. Intelligence Community
IRTPA	Intelligence Reform and Terrorism Prevention Act
LRIT	Long Range Identification and Tracking
MARAD	Maritime Administration
MDA	Maritime Domain Awareness
MSSIS	Maritime Safety and Security Information System
MOTR	Maritime Operational Threat Response (Plan)
MSIPC	Maritime Security Interagency Policy Committee
MSWG	Maritime Security Working Group
NAIS	Nationwide Automatic Identification System
NIEM	National Information Exchange Model
NIPP	National Infrastructure Protection Plan
NMDAP	National Maritime Domain Awareness Plan
NMIO	National Maritime Intelligence-Integration Office
NOAA	National Oceanic and Atmospheric Administration
NPAMDA	National Plan to Achieve Maritime Domain Awareness
NSGSCS	National Strategy for Global Supply Chain Security
NSISS	National Strategy for Information Sharing and Safeguarding
NSMS	National Strategy for Maritime Security
NSS	National Security Staff or National Security Strategy

ODNI	Office of the Director of National Intelligence
PM-ISE	Program Manager-Information Sharing Environment
PPD	Presidential Policy Directive
PPI	Personally Identifiable Information
SOLAS	Safety of Life at Sea
SILO	Single Integrated Lookout list
S/L/T/T	State, Local, Tribal, and Territorial (governments and agencies)
USCG	United States Coast Guard

APPENDIX E: REFERENCES

Chairman of the Joint Chiefs of Staff, *Joint Vision 2020* (June 2000).

Executive Order Number 13547; *Stewardship of the Ocean, Our Coasts, and the Great Lakes* (July 19, 2010).

Homeland Security Act of 2002, Pub. L. No. 107-296, 116 Stat. 2135 (November 25, 2002).

Intelligence Community Directive 208, *Write for Maximum Utility* (December 2008).

Intelligence Community Directive 209, *Tearline Production and Dissemination* (September 2012).

Intelligence Community Directive 902, *Global Maritime and Air Intelligence Integration* (January 14, 2009).

Intelligence Reform and Terrorism Prevention Act of 2004, Pub. L. No. 108-458 (December 17, 2004).

Joint Publication 2-0, *Joint Intelligence* (June 22, 2007).

National Infrastructure Protection Plan: Partnering to Enhance Protection and Resiliency (2009).

National Security Act of 1947, 50 U.S.C.A. §§ 401 et seq. (July 26, 1947).

National Security Strategy (May 2010).

National Strategy for Global Supply Chain Security (January 2012).

National Strategy for Information Sharing: Successes and Challenges in Improving Terrorism-Related Information Sharing (October 2007).

National Strategy for Information Sharing and Safeguarding (December 2012).

National Strategy for Maritime Security (September 2005).

Office of the Director of National Intelligence, *Strategic Plan (2012-15)*.

Presidential Policy Directive 1 / (PPD-1): *Organization of the National Security Council System* (February 13, 2009).

Presidential Policy Directive 4 (PPD-4): *National Space Policy* (June 29, 2010).

Presidential Policy Directive 18 / (PPD-18): *Maritime Security* (August 14, 2012).

Presidential Policy Directive 21 / (PPD-21): *Critical Infrastructure Security and Resilience* (February 12, 2013).

Uniting and Strengthening America by Providing Appropriate Tools Required to Intercept and Obstruct Terrorism Act, Pub. L. No. 107-56, 115 Stat. 272 (October 26, 2001).

The National Strategy for Maritime Security

National Maritime Domain Awareness Plan

Maritime Operational Threat Response Plan

International Outreach and Coordination Strategy

The Maritime Infrastructure Recovery Plan

Maritime Transportation System Security Plan

The Maritime Commerce Security Plan

The Domestic Outreach Plan

www.ingramcontent.com/pod-product-compliance
Lightning Source LLC
Chambersburg PA
CBHW080633290526
45790CB00007B/3051